arena

portfolios

Arena would like to acknowledge the help and assistance of the following people without whose contribution this publication would not have been possible.

Joan Wakelin's estate for the generous financial contribution.
Eva and Tony Worobiec for the enormous task of editing.
Harminder Singh and Nick Cooper for preparing Trevor Crone's and Kirsten Cooke's text.
Steve Gubbins for supplying Colin Westgate's portrait.

Design and layout by Ted Sturgeon

Printed by Berforts Limited, Hastings, East Sussex

Published by ARENA Publications 2008

ISBN 978-0-9559059-0-2

Cover: Joan Wakelin

Arena was founded in 1986 by Joan Wakelin together with a group of young photographers, largely from the Newbury area, who wanted to create a free-thinking open forum for like-minded photographers in the south of England. The concept had been inspired initially by the internationally known Kontiki group, and also by Gamma, a group based in the north of the country. The formula was a simple one: that members bring along their work and offer it up for discussion. Another key aim was to attract Britain's finest contemporary photographers as speakers.

Although the original group numbered just 15 members, it was decided in the mid 1990s to expand to nearly double that. However, a resolution was made very early on in the history of Arena that membership would be by invitation only and this has been strictly maintained. For the first 15 years, members regularly met at The Newbury Arts Workshop, before transferring to the Elizabethan mansion of Ufton Court near Reading.

Exhibiting together has been another important part of Arena's philosophy. In the 1990s it participated in an ambitious themed exhibition entitled *North/South* with its sister group Gamma at The National Museum Of Photography in Bradford. It also organized another themed exhibition, *"Routes",* which was shown at the Barbican, London. Members' work has been further showcased in the capital, notably at Bishopsgate, Whiteleys and Hays Galleria. Additional group exhibitions have been held in Reading, Poole, Salisbury and Guildford.

The current aims of Arena have not changed in its 22 year history; they are to promote the highest standards in photography, and to encourage printmaking. Members are expected to bring work to each meeting to be critically appraised by fellow Arena colleagues. Joan's original philosophy was to "to applaud those working at the frontiers of photo development, to search and discover ourselves and find fulfillment", and this remains our central tenet today. Arena is best known for its annual seminar which is also open to non-members. The purpose of the seminar is to invite the finest photographers in the country to share their work with the group, a tradition which Arena has every intention of continuing.

This publication has been produced in memory of Joan Wakelin, who died in 2003, but it is also a celebration of the wonderful diversity of the work of Arena members. All, in their different ways have achieved at the highest level and these images represent the best contemporary photography from the south of England. Many of its members have had individual portfolios of their work published while others lead very successful workshops, both in the UK and abroad. I sincerely hope that you will gain great pleasure from this book; if you wish to know anything further about Arena, please visit our website at *www.arenaphotographers.com.*

Enjoy!

Tony Worobiec (Chairman)

arena

Joan Wakelin was the inspiration behind Arena; a passionate photographer, she recognized that nowhere within the south of England was there a forum where photographers from a broad spectrum of photography could meet regularly to show and discuss their work. She felt as a photojournalist that she did have something to offer a fine-art photographer and vice versa. She also promoted a climate of healthy debate within Arena and constantly encouraged constructive criticism within the group. Initially she invited 15 participants from the Newbury area, but steadily opened up the group to include photographers from across the entire region. Despite a long illness, Joan continued to be an inspirational and active member of Arena right up until her death in 2003.

Joan was born in Lancashire and started taking photographs at the age of 10. Initially she concentrated on her immediate environment, on the industrial scenes and people working within those communities. In her youth she briefly trained as a portrait photographer and quickly acquired an almost instinctive appreciation of lighting. But Joan had a passion for travel and from this she quickly became interested in the human condition. A moral and principled person, she felt she simply could not ignore much of the poverty and hardship she was witnessing and felt she needed to bring this to the attention of a wider audience; this became her quest in life. Joan was also extremely resourceful in being able to photograph in particularly difficult situations. She famously kept her camera concealed in a knitting-bag, anxious always not to draw attention to herself. Disciplining herself to use just two or three lenses, her work retains a directness and spontaneity. She really knew how to engage with people; allied to her warmth and humour she had the capacity to capture truly iconic images. As age caught up with her and her ability to travel was restricted, she decided to look much closer to home. In her seventies and living just a

stone's throw from a lively haunt in the heart of Bath, Joan had the savvy, charm and ability to produce a wonderfully incisive portfolio on the clubbing culture. Her appetite for photography remained insatiable.

As a photojournalist, Joan will be best remembered for her black and white images.

Although she was involved with many notable projects, perhaps the two that were closest to her heart were the studies of the New Zealand's Maori and Australian Aboriginal communities; in typical self-deprecation she famously said "They thanked God for me being there but probably thanked him when I had gone". In photographing the tragic circumstances of the Vietnamese boat people in 1989 she felt that she had reached the peak of her career and was deservedly included in the 1990 World Press Awards. She was made an honorary Fellow of the Royal Photographic Society in 1992 and the British Institute of Photography. The RPS also bestowed on her the coveted Fenton Medal.

In the 1990s she settled down to a more sedate life in Berkshire but still managed to find interesting subjects to photograph. Despite her illness she characteristically embraced the digital era, and some of her most striking work was done at the very end of her life. A broad selection of her work is currently in the RPS archives at the National Museum of Film, Photography and Television, Bradford.

portfolio of work

joan wakelin

Aboriginal, Cherbourg, Australia (1998)

Nancy, Aboriginal Community, Australia

T's Nightclub, Bath

As a young man, Bob Elliott trained as a draughtsman, although secretly he had always harboured a desire to become a journalist, but his father convinced him that he ought to go into something more secure. He joined The Ordnance Survey, where his many skills were very quickly recognized, first as a draughtsman, then as a surveyor, when he was put in charge of surveyors in the south of England. He was viewed by his employers as someone who was capable, flexible and adaptable, so when they were looking for someone to take over the newly created digital section, Bob was a natural choice. He gained a reputation for clarity of thought, excellent organization and communicational skills and consequently was highly respected by all his colleagues. Not surprisingly, he brought many of these skills to his photography.

An exceptional craftsman, he excelled as a print-maker; he was a talented darkroom worker who truly understood that the negative has the potential to express his own personal ideas, thoughts and emotions. It was often remarked that Bob could truly "make a silk purse from a sow's ear." Always aware of new developments, he was one of the first monochrome specialists to make the transition from darkroom to lightroom, and typically, having acquired these new skills, Bob was always generous with his time helping others make the change.

While Bob had produced several colour images, his real passion was for monochrome. He had an innate visual understanding of the emotive value of tones and would expertly manufacture his images to create the maximum emotional impact. A quiet and sometimes private man, he always retained a cultured sense of humour that regularly appears in his work. He was also fascinated by the Surrealists and would often produce witty and visually stunning composites.

But Bob's real passion was for travel, and it was perhaps these experiences that inspired his most memorable work. He spent part of his national service in Kenya where he witnessed first hand many of the injustices that were committed at the time. A passionate admirer of Sebastiao Salgado, Bob has always had a concern for the human condition, and this became more evident as he got older. Visiting countries as diverse as Cuba, China, the USA, Thailand and South Africa, he refused to travel with his eyes closed and wanted to highlight injustice wherever he saw it. Blessed with natural charm, he had a genuine empathy with people, and when he photographed poverty, his subjects instinctively knew that this was not the work of a voyeurist, but someone who really cared for their plight. Even when traveling through Europe, Bob sought to illustrate aspects of the human condition which many of us unwittingly ignore.

It perhaps significant that through his photography, Bob became the journalist he always wished to be.

portfolio of work

bob elliott

Sikh Parade

Lowry at the Tate Modern

Florence, Langa Township, South Africa

Langa Township, South Africa

Edward Sturgeon is a people photographer. His passions encompass dance, portraits in the studio and on location, some wild and empty landscape pictures and, more recently, a major project with a distinctly historical flavour. Most of his art follows his own interests and instincts but the occasional commission gives him added challenges.

As befits the times we live in, his media include colour, monochrome, film and digital. He is an accomplished darkroom worker and continues to develop, print and finish in his own darkroom in parallel with the now inevitable computer screen and printer. In addition to his own photography, he helps other photographers in workshop sessions whenever his full time job as a graphic design studio manager allows it.

Edward started to take photographs whilst studying Graphic Design at college, a choice then dictated by his poor health during childhood. Initially the pictures were only those that his design education required, but after a period he started to experiment. It was then that he discovered black and white, both film and printing. It opened up a whole new visual area to explore and he went on to make many types of picture, both graphic and for personal interest.

Although he enjoyed simple photography, he was often frustrated by the challenge of conveying his thoughts and feelings with just a single image and so he started producing groups of pictures to tell a story. Around the same time, he was approached to take some photographs for the college's fashion show. Despite initial reservations, Edward found that he enjoyed this branch of photography and now continues making many different types of people pictures. It was from this fortuitous beginning that his current series works are derived.

In Edward's dance photography series, the images combine the gracefulness of the ballerina and the feeling of light, air and movement. Initially the pictures were produced traditionally by overexposing Konica Infra Red film and printing the image in the darkroom to a high key finish. This ensured that the delicacy and the beauty of the movement were captured but not thrust in ones face. The results encouraged repeated and lengthy viewing, allowing the image to materialise before the viewer's eyes. Edward's dance series has now been expanded to take advantage of modern digital technology. Manipulating the image and combining more than one original to produce a much more subtle result has succeeded in conveying the sense of movement more freely. The viewer is thus transported into a realm of fantasy, yet can still see the reality.

The series of Second World War images evolved from a long-held interest in this poignant part of our history. Throughout the country there are many meetings, gatherings and events that specialise in reliving some aspects of that era. The participants take extreme care that all material such as vehicles and clothing is true to those times. Although many modern items are present, Edward was keen to exclude them, ensuring that the pictures have the authentic look of the period. For the first tranche of pictures he printed traditionally on a matt paper that was then tinted (in cold tea!) to produce an older feel. Once these were made, he experimented with other darkroom techniques and materials until trying the digital option. It was here that he found the key to producing a series of montage images that gave the viewer some feeling of what life looked like during WWII, and more importantly to those who actually had been there, being able to recognise and relive the visual experience.

No doubt these and other projects will evolve over the years – *why should art stand still?* – and Edward will certainly complement them with other equally ambitious future works.

portfolio of work

edward sturgeon

Dance

The Yanks are here!

Evacuation

Dave Mason describes his involvement in photography as a constant passion. He looks upon his photography as a very private and somewhat personal experience, both while capturing the image and during the printing of it. However, he also enjoys sharing the final images with others, through publications, exhibitions and by giving illustrated talks.

Over the years Dave has experimented with and recorded all types of subject matter, in colour and monochrome, producing images ranging from detailed, intimate close-ups and still life through to grand panoramic land and seascapes. He looks upon this period of experimentation as an exploratory time, a precursor to finding his niche.

Dave believes that in recent years he has found his place in photography and now concentrates chiefly on the urban environment, its inhabitants and its textures. His enjoyment of this subject matter is due to its random nature: the unpredictable combination of the constantly changing backdrop – whether it is buildings, posters, hoardings, etc - , the changing light – whether it is natural or ambient – and of course the passing strangers.

Dave approaches street photography in a very different manner to those whose names instantly spring to mind when street photography is mentioned – Henri Cartier-Bresson, Elliott Erwitt and Gary Winogrand. For these great photographers it was very much about capturing the moment or, to use the classic Cartier Bresson phrase, 'the decisive moment'. Dave however prefers first to find an interesting backdrop and then wait for the 'actors' (passing strangers) to appear. One could compare him to a theatre director, except that in this case the 'actors' decide on their own movements on the 'stage'.

Among his influences Dave includes the film director and photographer Wim Wenders for his use of saturated light and colour, the photographer Stephen Shore for recording the ordinary and often bland places of America with such expert precision, and the legendary Lee Friedlander for his ability to make personal order out of chaos.

Perhaps his strongest influence is Joel Meyerowitz, whose early colour images of the streets of New York are for Dave a constant reference point and inspiration. It is with this iconic set of images in mind that Dave had the idea of the 'Confused Corners'.

In the Confused Corners portfolio Dave concentrated on street scenes where a vast amount of information had been amassed, thus cluttering the environment and causing confusion. Dave further created a sense of confusion and chaos within the image by his selective disregard of the accepted concepts of photographic practice, such as the rules of composition.

Dave recalls a small piece of stencil graffiti he once read which he believes expresses how he feels about his photography:

'In life one can lose everything but one's passion'
Dave hopes to keep his passion alive.

portfolio of work

dave mason

Confused Corner 1

Confused Corner 2

Confused Corner 3

UK born documentary photographer Colin Summers stumbled upon photography as a serious medium whilst travelling in the Far East during his early 20's. He says "Naively I had managed to get into Cambodia during the UN controlled elections in 1993. The country was emerging from decades of war and I was privileged to be a witness to a small part of this change. I decided to record the events with a camera and this changed the way I looked at photography and travel. It motivated me and gave me a sense of direction. Being naturally curious, photography gave me the excuse to take a step closer."

Colin continued to travel throughout the Far East and India, taking his photography more and more seriously. Initially shooting with colour negative, he later switched to monochrome, finding this a more powerful means of expression. He prints his own images and says, "I'm really passionate about the whole process, from the original exposure through to the final print. The work in the darkroom is as important to me as taking the photograph. It keeps me in touch".

To date some of Colin's projects have included the opium problem in northern Laos, landmines and their effects on the Cambodian people, child trafficking and narcotics in Cambodia and the Asian tsunami from the worst affected area Banda Aceh, Indonesia. "I'm really fascinated by people's lives and have a huge amount of respect for how people cope in different and sometimes terrible situations. I try, and I hope this is evident in my images, to convey the truth in a compassionate and inoffensive way".

The following three images were taken in the wake of the 2004 Boxing Day tsunami. On hearing the news Colin made the decision to travel to Sumatra (Indonesia), where he managed to join an aid convoy heading to the island's northern tip, Banda Aceh, situated 160km from the epicentre. The earthquake generated a tsunami with waves rising to heights in excess of 20 metres. On arrival, he was confronted by unimaginable scenes of destruction. One example was the small town of Leupueng, originally with a population of 10,000 but after the disaster reduced to less than 700. The town was completely obliterated. Colin says "just before 8 a.m on the 26th it was a bustling community preparing for the day but by 8.30 the town had been erased. When the photographs were taken, it was eerily quiet, the only human reference being the pungent smell hanging in the hot, humid air". Over 800km of coastline had been destroyed, 200,000 lives lost and 1/2 million people left homeless in Aceh alone. "During the time I spent in Aceh I witnessed a strength and dignity born of a faith and culture wholly unlike my own. I found the experience challenging and humbling".

portfolio of work

colin summers

A teacher of art, Tony Worobiec bought his first camera ostensibly to introduce topic work to his students; however, an interest in photography for its own sake quickly developed and has since become an all-consuming passion. Nevertheless, he has long been concerned by the limitations that photography imposes, and was frustrated by how very little it seemed to have progressed since its inception in the middle of the 19th century.

A breakthrough came with the development of digital imaging. Initially his response was guarded, but he then began to appreciate the immense scope this new medium offers. As a painter, he felt that starting with a "blank canvas" allowed him to fully impose himself on the image, although achieving this through photography had been much harder. By starting with a new file using Photoshop, it is now possible to import a variety of sources (not all necessarily photographic) and weave them together into a highly personal visual statement. The work of the American Pop artist Robert Rauschenberg proved to be inspirational and in particular his clever use of the visual analogy. Tony is also a great admirer of the photographer Olivia Parker whose work has greatly expanded his understanding of the medium.

Creating images using a flatbed scanner has proven to be especially liberating. Firstly it allows him to capture fragments that normally one would choose to discard. The obvious choices are small natural objects such as feathers, cones, leaves and so on, but it is also possible to fuse these with a variety of other unrelated elements: detritus, jottings, maps or crumpled pieces of paper for example. Photographing these still-lifes has never been an attempt to dispassionately record specifics, but rather to evoke something more ephemeral. He seeks not always to communicate at an intellectual level, but rather to appeal to a common, subliminal subconscious. Using even a modest resolution, seemingly inconsequential elements can assume an entirely new identity, revealing an astonishing wealth of detail. He tries to make these "captures" as simple as possible, so that other elements can be woven into the final composite. Backgrounds are often derived from colour photographs taken of abandoned or distressed vehicles. What particularly interests him is using elements that vary in scale, emanating from a variety of sources which can be presented either as a positive or a negative. He frequently fuses the original scanned image with an inverted background, employing this as the basis of the composite.

The structure of the final image is important. Using highly disparate elements, Tony tries to ensure that the overall design remains simple; using a visual palindrome is a simple case in point. For ideas, he usually dips into examples of abstract painting (or even folk art) and then carefully works his selected elements into the final composition. Often asked how certain "effects" are achieved, Tony admits that he is unsure. When creating these composites he tries not to start with a pre-conceived idea and by applying numerous adjustment layers he is able to experiment with a variety of options, reacting only as the image emerges. As each layer is introduced, the composition enters a new phase of its metamorphosis, requiring careful and thoughtful reflection. He steadfastly refuses to save the sequence in Actions, because he believes that what works well with one composite will not necessarily work with another.

portfolio of work

tony worobiec

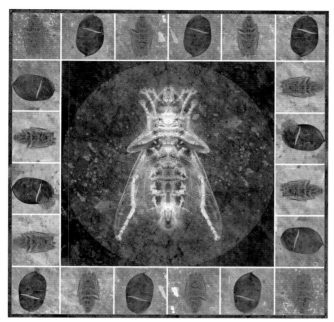

Fly

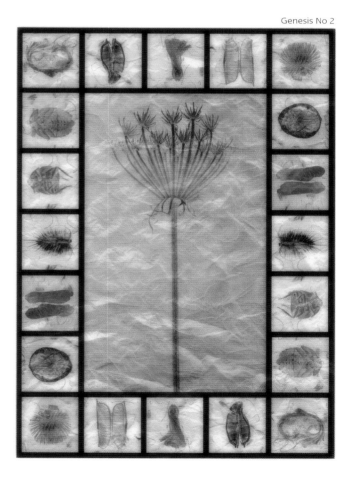

Genesis No 2

Teasel

Lakota

Caroline entered the world of photography when, at the age of 18, she started to work as an assistant to a fashion photographer in London. She soon progressed to taking portfolios round to the top advertising agencies for new accounts and became more involved with the actual studio photography.

Having learnt a lot about cameras, film and lighting, she was keen to start taking photographs herself and evolved a lifelong passion which was further stimulated by an entry in the 1981 London Salon which led to a one-woman show later that year in the capital.

Caroline finds working with natural subjects inspirational, as one is forced to look at minute detail that might normally go unnoticed. Much of her subject matter consists of *'objets trouvés'* found on random walks on a country lane or in surrounding woods in Oxfordshire near her home and studio, with an occasional 'discovery' on an overseas trip.

Whilst elements such as dried leaves, fish skeletons and even animal's skulls have proven to be a rich source of subject matter for Caroline's images, she is particularly drawn towards wild flowers, due to their depth of colour and the fact that, as they tend to be small, they require much careful study.

Working with still lives and with flowers, she is a photographer with a refined sense of shape, form and light. Everything is captured on black and white film, archivally printed on fibre-based paper, then toned in sepia, selenium or gold. Some images are then hand tinted. The process is lengthy and time consuming but the end result evokes the warm colours of nature. Caroline is often asked why she doesn't just use colour film, but she believes that hand coloured and toned photographs appear to have a much richer quality, making the final print well worth the hours spent on it.

Caroline Hyman's talent lies not only in the mastery of the technical process but also her ability to inspire the subject matter with a poetic vision that is very much her own, maintaining her high standards coupled with exquisite grace and elegance of vision. She believes that we are all surrounded by an endless supply of still life material and that it isn't always necessary to travel to distant lands in order to make original and interesting photographs.

Her recent work has been influenced by the botanical drawings of the Victorian era and involves detailed observations of hedgerow plants, arums, wild violets, dandelions and bluebells. The beauty of wild flowers that so often go unnoticed is given prominence here resulting in prints which are simple and uncluttered: the roots and corms are seen, alongside buds, seed pods, petals and leaves. Plain backgrounds and soft lighting emphasise the unique quality of each plant.

Caroline's work is widely exhibited and held in public and private collections around the world. Her gift for capturing the fragile reality and fading beauty of the natural world was reflected in a comment on her work by photographer Terry O'Neill:

"... A stunning, fresh, innovative eye in photography – the Georgia O'Keefe of the camera."

portfolio of work

caroline hyman

Arum

Chives

Grape Hyacinth

Carol first trained in Fine Art as a painter. However, it was taking record photographs of her paintings with a digital camera that drew her towards photography. The ability to take a photograph, develop it with appropriate software and print out the desired result proved compulsive; she has never looked back.

As her interest in photography grew, she found herself drawn to artists and photographers who worked in themes, often related to natural forms. John Blakemore's beautiful tonal images of tulips, Georgia O'Keefe's larger than life sensual flowers and Karl Blossfeldt's bold, tactile work of architectural plant forms, were all inspirational. Having enjoyed these particular qualities in the images of others, she now strives to produce them within her own work.

For Carol there are clear correlations between photography and painting. She uses the camera as a tool for composition, structure and form in a way similar to using a brush or pencil for a painting. Whether painting or taking a photograph, she enjoys the process of slowing down and taking time out to contemplate on the chosen subject matter. Whilst arranging the still life, she waits until an emotional response to the light, space and composition is experienced before beginning work. Many of the images have a centred, upright composition using simple forms, as these evoke a sense of stillness and time, which is very much missing in our busy everyday life.

Carol has a passion for flower photography. The gladioli, tulip and delphinium are personal favourites. The first images she produced were inspired by tulips with their colourful shapes and graceful forms which often convey a theatrical quality. To enhance the colourful aspect of these flowers she painted separate backgrounds for each one to portray this vision of the tulip. This approach emphasized the theatrical quality she responded to, and also brought painting and photography together in one image.

In a later series of images, flowers were arranged and photographed to suggest the underlying impression of a female figure. This was accomplished through working with several layers in software, using both photographic and painted images, to produce this symbolic image of the female form. Her aim was to celebrate the beauty, femininity and symbolism of the female using 'Nature's Gems' as the Victorians called them.

Printing is very much part of the creative process and her preference is for Hahnemuehle Photo Rag or Arches watercolour paper. Although the latter is more difficult to print and can produce a much flatter, less colourful image, she likes the challenge of this archival art paper. Carol rarely paints now, as photography is her main artistic medium, but drawing is still valued as a discipline. She finds the hands-on experience of drawing on paper and working tonally with charcoal retains both eye and hand co-ordination, adding to her ongoing growth and experience as a photographer and artist.

portfolio of work

carol hicks

John is self-taught, with an enthusiastic passion for monochrome photography. By and large he finds considerable inspiration in the works of the Photo-Secession movement which was established in the United States in the early years of the 20th century. Workers such as Steiglitz and Langdon Coburn, to name just two of the many advocates of that movement, and more lately the Spanish photographers Echagüe and Ortiz provide much of the stimulation for the style of his work. What he finds appealing about these photographs is the often misused term 'pictorialism' in that they emphasise the emotional tonality of the subject through the arrangement of shape, light and shade within the picture. He feels this invites the viewer to consider them akin to a musical tone poem rather than as an exercise in being able to count the number of blades of grass or grains of sand.

This outlook is exploited in John's work to give a unique view of the subjects he photographs. For example, in visiting a country for the first time he will create in his mind some idea of how he would like to convey his feelings about that place. His idiosyncratic views of Venice, provided in the accompanying photographs, have entailed a number of visits to that city to progress to the current stage. They attempt to show a Venice that is disintegrating slowly but is still nevertheless the grand lady of the Adriatic. Sadly, due to the impending climate change and despite all efforts to stop the decay, Venice will one day almost certainly disappear beneath the waves. January was the preferred month to take these photographs, mainly because it is less crowded, but also because of the beautiful soft low lighting at that time of year. However a word of advice - take some warm clothing, as it can get very cold in the winter months.

The Venice photographs have been taken on a 5x4 camera using Polaroid Type 55 film (which gives a black & white print and a useable negative) and using an Imagon soft-focus lens. The developed negatives were allowed to 'age' by deliberately not placing them in a clearing bath as normal. The result is that over time the negative will obtain a degree of random and uncontrolled 'distress'. Finally the prints were made using Forte Poly Warmtone paper 'lith' developed and either Selenium, Gold or sepia toned.

portfolio of work

john gould

Venice 1

Venice 2

Venice 3

Early in her journey into the magical world of photography, Kathy became intrigued by the creative potential that it offered, especially as a means of personal expression. Through both studying other people's work and by her own experimentation she realised that her interest lay in working with black and white film. The purity and simplicity of this medium was a strong factor in making this choice, coupled with her interest in darkroom work. Being able to control the evolution of the image from the moment the image was exposed to the moment she held the final picture in her hands captivated her.

She then moved on to experimenting with the use of infrared film, and found that the film's special characteristics perfectly matched the way she liked to interpret her subjects. Typically, soft, delicate ethereal images, with an almost transcendental quality became possible due to the extended sensitivity of this film. Though more difficult to handle than its panchromatic equivalent, it became a firm favourite, and to this day Kathy continues to explore its many facets and idiosyncrasies.

The majority of her pictures are unplanned; she prefers to work intuitively, responding to what she sees and feels. She strives not only to record the essence of a place but also to convey a more personal and creative impression of the subject, with reality giving way to her preferred vision. There is a strong element of pre-visualisation of the final image in the way she works.

For Kathy, choosing the moment of exposure is always important; she is constantly responsive to the ever-changing qualities of light around her and the interplay between this and her subject. Whether subtle or dramatic, she feels that small changes in the light breathe life, sensitivity and emotion into a picture.

Though the moment, the choice of subject, light and exposure are of great importance, a lot of the work towards getting back to that pre-visualised image is achieved through interpretation of the negative in the darkroom. Kathy uses a variety of beautiful fibre based papers and toners, and she often lith prints or hand colours her work to achieve the desired results.

Photography is a very important part of Kathy's life. The gift of seeing in a different way is the most important thing that she has gained from her involvement in photography. At times she looks at the world as a series of potentially powerful images and this can be exciting or distracting.

With so much yet to explore, master and enjoy, Kathy knows that photography will be a lifelong interest.

portfolio of work

kathy harcom

Serenity

Leaning Fence

Bridge to the Aviary

Carousel, Paris

Colin Westgate has lived in the country for most of his life and when he made his first explorations into photography in his early 20's, it was natural for him to turn to the landscape as his subject. His love and enthusiasm for this remains undiminished and he still experiences that wonderful feeling of reverence and excitement when nature turns on the light and transforms the landscape into a vision of haunting beauty.

Initially, Colin photographed mostly in his home county of Sussex, but later he was able to travel further afield, in particular to the north of England and to Scotland, where the mountain scenery gave him inspiration for more dramatic interpretations. Landscape photography is as much about *feeling* as it is about seeing and by use of contrast and tonal controls, he found monochrome a powerful medium for interpretation and expression.

Colin did, however, eventually move into colour, making Cibachrome (later Ilfochrome) prints from slides. This required a different way of thinking and was, in many ways, more challenging. As a result, he sometimes employed methods such as diffusion and fast, grainy film to modify the literal quality that colour gave. This suppression of fine detail often resulted in an ethereal, impressionistic effect, and once again allowed room for interpretation.

With the development of digital photography, the scope for expression in both colour and monochrome increased enormously, and the fine controls available enhance the ability of the photographer to make full use of his or her creative vision. Colin embraced this to the full, but feels there is a danger of the software providing an easy method of making material and structural changes to a picture.

For Colin, taking a landscape photograph can be very emotional and what he calls 'the integrity of the experience' is very important. The excitement of the light and mood, the wind on the face, the exhilaration of pressing the shutter at a precise moment, are all part of an experience he tries to convey in his pictures. Adding or removing elements, or changing a composition by altering their position, can significantly modify the original image. While the result may be 'stronger' in some respects, the experience of the moment of taking is corrupted and the satisfaction of producing the picture diminished. This is, of course, a paradox, as monochrome photography in particular is very much a manipulative process. But as we do not literally see in monochrome, Colin considers that interpretative controls, whether used in the darkroom or digitally, are a valid part of the process of the putting onto the paper the original *vision* that a 'straight' print from a negative or file could not achieve. There is a real difference between this and altering the material structure of the image.

It has often been suggested that Colin romanticises the landscape – but he makes no apologies for this! Mankind has always had an impact on the landscape and sometimes changed it irrevocably for the worse, but it has always been Colin's aim to unashamedly portray the intrinsic beauty of the subject, whether it is a detailed and colourful structure of a rock or the wonder of a magnificent scene. For Colin, the landscape is a very spiritual place, to be respected, cherished and enjoyed.

In the six pictures that follow, Colin has sought to portray the various stages and styles of his photographic journey.

portfolio of work

colin westgate

Seaweed & Rock (2003)

Poppies, Spain (1986)

Misty Day, Seven Sisters (2001)

Dune Abstract (1999)

Downland Track (1973)

Lone Tree (2005)

It takes only one look at the pictures adorning the walls of Yeovil photographer Kirsten Cooke's home to tell you that she has an uncommon approach to her art. Not only are the subjects themselves diverse, but her style often varies between the different types of photographs she takes, or the recording medium she uses. In fact, the camera itself is only one part of Kirsten's story. "I was a fine artist before I was a photographer. I approach everything from an artistic base, rather than a technical one," explains Kirsten, who was educated in Somerset before going on to Goldsmiths to study for her degree. "I was there at a time when technology was very basic and we played around with translating photographs onto silk screens and printing fabric from them. So I started using my camera as an extension of myself, like a pencil or a paintbrush. I have always viewed my camera as a tool and a means to an end, rather than just something that produces images."

Kirsten returned to college to improve her darkroom skills. She has a particular fascination with photographing people within their environment and, by the second year of the five-year course, which led to her becoming an Associate of the Royal Photographic Society, found that her skills were in such demand that photography soon became her career.

The eclectic mix of artists whose work she admires helps to explain Kirsten's broad-ranging approach to her own work. The photographers among them have mainly come to the medium from an art base, rather than a technical one. Her list includes photographers like Roger Fenton and Cecil Beaton, perhaps noted for a formality of style and attention to detail in black and white portraiture, as well as painters and sculptors, ranging from Caravaggio, Rembrandt and Vermeer, to Kandinsky, Moore and Hepworth.

Although she will sometimes use a digital camera, by far the majority of Kirsten's photographic work is done with film, involving her in the darkroom processes which she enjoys. The choice of medium she uses, either colour or black and white film, often has quite a bearing on her finished work, too. Her black and white photography often has a measured, classical quality. If taking a portrait, for instance, she might spend much time talking to the subject, paying meticulous attention to the details of the surroundings, before pressing the shutter and getting her shot, just as the photographers she admires might have done. "When I take portraits, I like them to tell a story and make a statement about the person at that point in time," says Kirsten. Her approach to colour photography, on the other hand, often produces results which are more abstract, more modernist, in nature. She admits to being more purist about black and white photography than about colour . "With colour, I like to allow myself time to let my mind wander and to push the boundaries."

As well as exhibiting a couple of times each year and lecturing to other photographers around the country, Kirsten teaches photography part-time at Yeovil College and has recently taken a year out to complete her MA in Fine Art Photography. "It was very exciting and gave me the opportunity for self-exploration, to translate ideas and to take my photography to another level," enthuses Kirsten.

portfolio of work

kirsten cooke

Carolyn and Guy

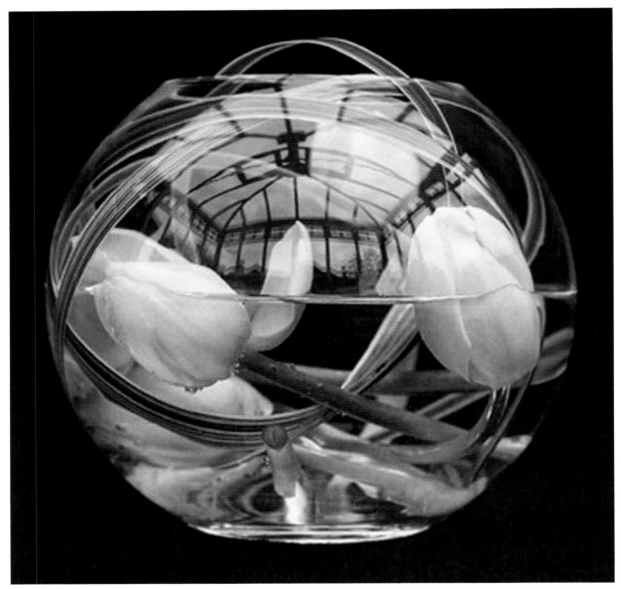

Florist Charlotte

Blue Bottle

Although Hugh's background is in science and technology, he was drawn towards photography in his early 30s. Gradually the interest grew into a serious hobby and then with family and work pressures easing, it became a passion and a way of life.

Initially, he concentrated on landscape monochrome photography, mainly making his own prints in the darkroom. With his continuing drive for perfection, he became a fine printer, carefully controlling the tonality and key of a print to capture the atmosphere inherent in the landscape.

Hugh's work ranges from studies of the wide-open landscape to intimate close-up details. It is in the latter that he finds immense satisfaction; these are the subjects that most people walk past without seeing, let alone appreciating them. Here is a wealth of subject matter: the delicate colours of rocks in the inter-tidal zones, the intriguing shapes of sand patterns on the sandy beaches, the assorted shapes and colours of fallen leaves and the detailed structure and colours of lichens.

With no formal training in art, he learnt about arrangement and design, quality of light and tonality by avidly reading and studying the work of other photographers. But the biggest change and influence was to come with the introduction of the computer. He had experimented with colour printing but felt frustrated by the lack of control and variability of the colour printing process. Even though labelled as 'computer illiterate' during his working days, he quickly became adept at using the new technology to obtain consistently the requisite colour harmonies that he had previously been unable to achieve.

Hugh has moved seamlessly from his earlier monochrome work to the present delicate colour images. Here we also see the influence of his love of watercolours and their subtle understated colours that he feels are relevant to the Northern landscape. He uses 35mm cameras and nowadays exclusively digital capture. Shooting with extreme wide-angle lenses (down to 12mm), he is able to concentrate on arrangements of foreground detail, which show some individuality in composition. Other images concentrate on simple, almost minimalist compositions that give broad washes of colour which provide the prevailing mood of the image.

He has photographed most notable locations in Britain and Southern Ireland and has a particular passion for the extensive beaches that lie along the west coast of Scotland and Ireland. It is a changing landscape, each day having a different mood and character.

In common with many photographers, Hugh enjoys the feeling of space and solitude that the landscape offers. There is an empathy and understanding of the changing moods, the delicacy and contrast of the light and a deep appreciation of the subtlety of colours that abound in the natural world. These are the qualities which he hopes to convey in his collections of images.

portfolio of work

hugh milsom

Trevor looks away as he presses the shutter ... this is the essence of his philosophy on registering an image, and to understand this we need to walk his path to the point of shutter release.

The basics first – Trevor's approach is to use the minimum technology which is necessary to achieve the final image. A subtle aspect of technology is how it shapes our behaviours and ultimately the images we record. The use of a 5x4 large format camera is not just about the quality it can produce; the detail and delineation of tones in Trevor's images is breathtaking and the edge demarcation of elements within the photograph gives a palpable sense of solidity and delicacy.

The view camera also slows down the picture taking process and leads to a contemplative approach. This is a key decision in Trevor's choice of technology and, as such he favours wide angle lenses, as they give him a better feeling of 'place'.

A photograph can be of the instance or it can capture the passage of time and Trevor excels at this. The use of small lens apertures and neutral density filters enables Trevor to use long time exposures -a few seconds to several minutes – which helps in communicating the haunting beauty of the landscape, as he sees it.

From his 'Coastal Fragments' portfolio, Trevor's photograph's of the disappearing world of bathing pools exquisitely captures both their decay and decadence. The position of these bathing pools at the edge of oceans suggest the tension of harnessing nature but in doing so losing some of the danger as well. These images operate at different levels and Trevor's images provide not only the enjoyment of aesthetics but a deeper pleasure in the way his photographs make us explore our own inner landscapes.

This brings us back to turning away at the point of release . . . and that is what is happening: a release or escape from the creative process by ending in a creative act. Turning his back to the image he is photographing gives the landscape a dignity by making it part of the creative act. And the act is both an end point and also a beginning to the realisation of the image through the creative workshop process. All the images are produced on Silver Halide paper which gives Trevor a physical and emotional connection to the emergence of the image which is both exhausting and exhilarating.

Images start from within and in Trevor's own words:

Eventually the process becomes intuitive and a form of meditation takes hold. The subject's form, texture, the light which it reflects; all these you feel as well as see. It is during such moments that completeness is felt; one is reluctant to leave the subject. You feel you have witnessed something special, something magical.

Trevor is a witness and his photography is evidence of the deepest connection to our changing British landscape.

portfolio of work

trevor crone

Bathing Pool, Broadstairs

Bathing Pool, Cliftonville

Bathing Pool, Minnis Bay

Tim Rudman was invited to join Arena in 1987, the year after the group had formed.

He works with black and white materials in the traditional darkroom and currently he most frequently uses toning and/or Lith printing techniques to interpret his images. His work has been widely exhibited around the world, gaining many awards and is represented in numerous private and permanent collections. He has authored four books on monochrome darkroom printing, toning and Lith printing and his writings and images have been widely published in books and magazines in many countries.

Tim's interest in photography began whilst studying medicine in the 1960s and was inspired by a book of graphic black and white images by the South African photographer Sam Haskins. This he recalls as his 'road to Damascus' moment, when he knew that monochrome photography would replace graphite and charcoal as the medium for his artistic expression. He located a darkroom, taught himself the basics of black and white printing and a lifelong love of photography was born.

Always primarily interested in monochrome, Tim's earlier photographic work sought to explore the play of light on form and as such was largely contre-jour, graphic and cold in tone. As it evolved, images were often constructed in the darkroom from several negatives. His other early influences came from the Pictorialist movement, for their use of image-altering techniques, and from Eugene Smith, for his use of dark tones and printing controls to direct the viewer's response.

His work took a new direction in the 1980s when he began to explore the then relatively under-documented process of Lith printing. By exploiting the unique characteristics of lith developer it is possible to produce on black and white paper images with a range of very warm tones and a mixture of coarse and fine grains. These produce high contrast in the shadows, together with soft creamy low contrast tones in the highlights. Both the colour and the tonal range of these prints can be manipulated and controlled by adjusting the exposure, the type of paper and the dilution, time and temperature of the developer.

Lith prints often look less photographically realistic than conventional black and white prints. Furthermore, as the process is very flexible and can produce an unusually wide range of effects, it allows the printer more creative freedom of expression. Tim exploits both of these virtues in his work and his use of chemical toners allows the introduction and control of a wider gamut of false colours. This not only abstracts the image further from reality but also allows him to influence spatial relationships within the print as well as the mood or atmosphere that is communicated to the viewer.

Although he does enjoy the succinctness of statement embodied in the single image, he also works extensively in themes, which may be tightly controlled or looser and self-directing over long periods of time. The images here come from a unique body of work on the derelict Victorian West Pier at Brighton, before it was destroyed by arson.

portfolio of work

tim rudman

Emergency Exit

As in Alfred Hitchcock's "The Birds" , the only occupants of the pier for a quarter of a century seemed to carry an air of menace, as they watched silently from every vantage point

Flight Path
Evidence of each successive occupation gradually overlays the previous ones! Sadly, in this case, all was subsequently lost to fire after two arson attacks

Starlings, railings and sunset
Noisy and gregarious, the starlings jostle for space in huge
numbers at sunset

Birds flocking before sunset

As the sun starts to go down, the peace and quiet at the end of the pier is shattered as the birds begin to collect in their tens of thousands

An engineer by training, Vic Attfield developed an interest in photography partially as an antidote to a very busy professional life. Whilst he has done a limited amount of colour work, he appears more comfortable when working in monochrome. A keen exhibitor in numerous national and international exhibitions, Vic's photographs are included in UK permanent collections such as The Tyng Collection of The Royal Photographic Society as well as in private collections in Russia and Europe.

Some contemporary exponents of street-photography argue that only by using colour is the photographer really able to present a true record. However Vic counters this by suggesting that all images are by their nature already one step from reality, as a photograph is simply a two dimensional interpretation of a three dimensional situation, therefore the decision whether to work in colour or black and white is largely irrelevant.

Vic contends that the camera is crucial as it allows us to record accurately everything around us. Being able to capture that critical instant in time is a facility Vic greatly values and is the primary reason for his passion for photography. He strongly maintains that the world around us is constantly changing and that the photographs he takes are a visual statement of our time. Moreover, he ardently believes that photographs can be taken in most situations, no matter how unpromising they may initially appear. Streets and towns reveal a challenging ebb and flow, which show humanity in varying and interesting situations. No two days are ever the same.

An essential ingredient to Vic's success is to keep everything simple. He uses a basic SLR with a built-in exposure meter and prefers to focus manually and set his own shutter speed and aperture. Using just three lenses, 28, 50 and 135mm, has over many years of experience allowed him to shoot almost without thinking, thus enabling him to concentrate more fully on the subject. Filling the frame is a crucial part of his photography. He applies the same simple logic to the production of his prints. After careful experimentation, Vic has established a combination of film, paper and chemical developers that best suit his own personal method of working.

Despite the unusual nature of so many of his photographs, it is important to appreciate that Vic's shots are hardly ever staged. In the spirit of Cartier-Bresson, a photographer Vic greatly admires, he tries to identify a promising scenario and waits to see what materializes. Nevertheless this still requires an instant decision, often allowing him time for just a single shot. Frequently needing to photograph unobserved, Vic elects never to work with a tripod and in order to overcome camera shake he habitually uses a 400 ASA film, which allows him to select a fast shutter speed.

When anticipating taking a photograph, Vic initially takes a meter reading and if the lighting situation allows, a shutter speed of 1/500 is selected. If using a 28mm lens, the focus is pre-set to 8 ft, which gives him sufficient depth of field for most eventualities. The 135mm lens is preset to about 20ft. As the lighting changes through the course of the day, readings are constantly taken and the necessary aperture adjustments made. By presetting in this way Vic is rarely if ever caught out, but if he sees a shot and suspects that the settings are not entirely appropriate, he will take it nevertheless; if he has time to make further aperture or focusing changes, then of course he will. At the heart of all of Vic's images is the simple but unwavering commitment to capture *the critical moment*.

portfolio of work

vic attfield

Children of Stratford

The Big Issue

Surf School

Department Store, Auckland, New Zealand

A trained linguist, Eva spent most of her working life as a teacher of languages, and took up photography as a corollary to work. Since her teenage years she always had a passionate interest in contemporary art, and much of her earlier photography was shaped by a fascination with bold areas of colour found in elements of landscape, industrial estates and seaside resorts.

Although initially working in colour slides, Eva gradually came to appreciate the greater subtlety offered by colour negative film. A change from using 35mm equipment to a Mamiya 645 system with its interchangeable backs led her to work more slowly and appreciate the higher quality which results from using a tripod on a regular basis. This way of working came to the fore in the extensive project which she shared with her husband, Tony, culminating in the publication, "Ghosts in the Wilderness: Abandoned America". This book documents the depleting communities of eastern Montana, western Nebraska, North and South Dakota and the Pawnee grasslands of Colorado.

In common with most Arena members, Eva derives greatest satisfaction from pursuing a photographic theme and has noticed that often a particular project develops organically and must have integrity. The images illustrated here on the theme of 'Icons of the Highway' initially emerged whilst finishing research for "Ghosts in the Wilderness" and noticing how rapidly the character of small town America was changing. Independent motels and cinemas in the central business districts, whose neon lights could often be seen from a mile away, were gradually being made redundant by large chain motel complexes on the Interstate exits or by multiplexes situated in out-of-town malls. Traditional cafes and diners, too, were losing out to the bevy of fast-food eateries which sprang up next to the new motels.

Thanks to the efforts of various groups and individuals, many of these traditional businesses are being kept alive, thus preserving an aspect of American culture which probably reached its heyday in the 1950s and 1960s, immortalized in the paintings of Edward Hopper and classic movies such as "American Graffiti". For the past three years Eva has been scouring the old American highways in search of these hauntingly beautiful places, capturing the dwindling glamour of many of the independent diners, motels, hotels, launderettes and theatres that continue to survive despite the odds.

Photographers who initially influenced Eva's approach were Joel Meyerowitz and Alfred Seiland, particularly the way in which they depicted the subtleties of twilight. She felt that these iconic places could be shown at their best in early evening when there is a crucial balance between the darkening sky and the neon lights; there was a definite decision to avoid as far as possible the near-black skies which often characterize so-called 'evening shots'. It soon emerged that the window of opportunity for such images could be as short as twenty minutes, and that a light meter and small torch were vital accessories. To allow for reciprocity failure, Eva had to bracket shots, but generally found that doubling the given exposure produced the best results. Where possible she chose to use a Fuji 6x9 rangefinder camera for the sheer quality of the final images.

Land of the Sun Cinema, Artesia

Blue Swallow Motel, Tucumcari

Hotel Monte Vista, Flagstaff

Roy has been deeply committed to photography for many years, and soon became aware of its unique qualities and the challenges presented. He prefers to photograph the ordinary everyday world that surrounds us, which he knows can be in turn chaotic, mundane, wonderful and mysterious. It is these very different characteristics which tend to inform and often inspire his work. He firmly believes that interesting and compelling images can be found almost anywhere, so long as one retains a receptive state of mind and avoids preconceived ideas.

Broadly speaking, Roy's favoured areas for working are urban and coastal locations. He is also drawn to certain landscapes, but usually the less obvious rather than naturally beautiful places. However, regardless of where he chooses to photograph, the one thing he considers most important is to convey a sense of place.

Looking for photographs so often relies on 'chance' happenings, and Roy fully believes that you need to be able to recognize these moments when they occur. There is an excitement about all this which he feels he thrives on. Photography is so often about special moments, and when these occur you need to be ready for them. Such a moment may demand a quick reaction if the subject is fleeting or transient, or, conversely, a more measured response if the subject is more static. The patience required not to move on too quickly and the ability to anticipate what might happen are other useful attributes.

Roy thinks that it is necessary when looking for pictures to be able to clear your mind of any other distractions and he heeds the words of the British photographer Raymond Moore about keeping a blank mind capable of receiving and giving. In order to tune himself in when beginning a day's work, Roy will often begin shooting off several frames on nothing in particular, so that he can kick-start the fragile but necessary coordination between mind, heart and eye.

A successful photograph, he believes, may well be an image that comes as something of a surprise, in that the viewer may not have visualized the picture in this way and therefore it will arouse their curiosity. Roy also thinks that a photograph does not necessarily have to explain everything and that a compelling image can be one that asks questions of the viewer.

Roy prefers to work in soft, gentle light – bright but not sunny. He is less happy with strong sunlight, but realizes that sometimes there is no choice and that it is important to be able to adapt. He has no problems with wet or overcast weather and believes that many good pictures arise out of such conditions, with a considerable gain in mood and atmosphere.

The work of many photographers has captured Roy's imagination and stimulated his thinking. Henri Cartier-Bresson, Robert Frank, Lee Friedlander, William Eggleston and Raymond Moore are just a few that have, in their very different ways, been an inspiration to him.

roy king *portfolio of work*

Isle of Sheppey, Kent

Barry Island, Wales

Prague, Czech Republic

When he was young George took up painting, first by sketching people, objects and places with pencil and watercolour, and later painting in oils. These disciplines were to prove their value much later when his artistic aims moved over to photography.

He was in the computer business and had been designing and programming computers for years when in 1958 he broke the world record for calculating π = 3.14159... to over 10,000 places. On his first overseas business trip he started to make colour slides of Canada and the USA to show to his family. Two years later he presented four papers at Australia's first computer conference, coming home via Tahiti, Hawaii and the USA – and taking more slides. Thus was born a passion which was to become of key importance in George's life.

He very much enjoys the whole experience of photography. His emotions are often stimulated when he looks at an interesting or dramatic scene, leading him to find a better view of the event, the street or the landscape and to make images reflecting his own interpretation. He uses his camera as often as possible; nowadays it is a digital one with several lenses and versatile controls. Although open to many photographic influences, he acknowledges the importance to him of the drama of images by Ansel Adams, Franco Fontana and many others. George also prefers stark landscapes of bare rock, mountains, lakes and waterfalls, and seeks to capture the often other-worldly nature of these places, especially those in good light.

He has travelled to many fascinating places which provided fertile inspiration for his photography, ranging from holidays in France, Spain and the Aegean to business journeys in South Africa, Canada, Sweden and the USA. From 1980 his trips included the American West, Iceland (six times), Norway, Greenland, Hawaii, Slovenia, New Zealand, Patagonia, Alaska and the Antarctic.

All these places have their own individual and very distinctive characteristics, seen not only in mountains, rivers, cities, volcanoes and forests, but also through the habits of the local people in their surroundings. In photographing these elements over the years, George has presented his interpretations through his images.

In 1976 he joined a photographic society where he learned the importance of hand printing. Then, in 1982, he bought a Leitz enlarger in order to make Cibachrome prints from his many colour slides. These prints had a very smooth mirror-glossy finish and needed careful processing. They taught him a great deal about making good prints, a skill which he was later able to transfer to the world of computer imaging with its powerful techniques.

An acknowledged perfectionist, George prepares his digital images for printing and projection with great care. In his computer he modifies them by careful adjustment of contrast and colour using Photoshop software. He insists that none of his photographs are published or exhibited without this treatment. Nowadays he has a state-of-the-art computer system which includes a professional printer built to prepare large high-quality archival prints.

Exotic landscapes are high in George's photographic interests – with occasional portraits and cityscapes. He is always pleased if he makes striking images of special or 'different' places, objects or viewpoints. The images in this portfolio are intended to show a few of his highlights.

portfolio of work

george felton

Rhyolite Mountains – this peak is called Reykjakollur and is in the hot-springs area of Landmannalaugur, famous for its yellow rhyolite mountains

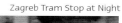

Zagreb Tram Stop at Night

Filling Station, Patagonia

Point Wild, Elephant Island

Paradise Harbour Sunset

Leigh has been involved in photography for 25 years, an interest which stems from his passion for art dating back to his school days. This gave him a grounding in the visual disciplines and in particular how tone, perspective and texture can influence the image. He uses the observed, the imagined and the constructed world as a vehicle for his own personal expression.

In order to research topics more deeply, Leigh often prefers to work in themes; he is well known for his series of emotive urban landscapes. He seeks to convey a sense of isolation by his careful use of scale and dramatic lighting. A feeling for the past endeavors of an industrial age and of forlorn subjects that are well past their sell-by date are recurring elements within his work. His motivation emanates from a sense of history as he rues the decline of once familiar skylines coupled with a desire to present the urban landscape afresh.

As tone plays such a major part of his work, he has largely restricted himself to monochrome. He particularly welcomes the control the wet darkroom offers as it allows him greater scope for his own creative inclinations. This brief portfolio reflects the world Leigh grew up in during the 1950s, half-remembered nostalgic scenes of an era which has been lost forever. Leigh's work has been influenced by the images of L S Lowry, Atkinson Grimshaw and the iconic photographs of Bill Brandt depicting satanic industrialization.

Taken just before sunrise, at twilight or at night, most of these images were captured in the dimly lit streets of northern England. Leigh prefers to use a medium speed film, (usually Ilford FP4), sets the lens for maximum depth of field, exposes for the highlights, but then develops the film to minimize contrast. This gives rise to the rich velvet blacks and the delicate highlight detail that are the hallmarks of so many of Leigh's prints. In order to match the mood of his printing with the starkness of the subject he often increases the contrast. He recognizes that this sometimes compromises shadow detail, but in order to affirm the artistic statement he prefers to leave it as an uncluttered, simple void.

Some photographers find working alone at night in an urban area or in poor weather unsettling, but Leigh believes it is this element that gives his images an "edge". Night and fog combine to obscure unwanted background distractions, evoking an eerie and timeless atmosphere. As long exposures are often required (some of Leigh's exposures are calculated in minutes rather than seconds), reciprocity needs to be overcome; he solves this by using a shutter speed which is twice as long as the metered reading. When using such lengthy exposures, wind can cause difficulties, particularly when longer lenses are being used: a heavy tripod is essential. Keen to balance the dark and lighter areas, Leigh sometimes chooses to use fill-in flash or even a torch to illuminate the impenetrable darker areas.

As there have been occasions when he has been questioned by the police, Leigh always carries some identification; he also suggests avoiding known trouble spots. His preferred time for taking his shots is just before total darkness in autumn and winter. As this falls earlier in the evening, it is likely to be much safer. Moreover, as the conditions are often damp and foggy at this time of year, that gritty film-noir style so wonderfully evoked by Carol Reed's "The Third Man" is more easily induced.

portfolio of work

leigh preston

Clitheroe

Gloucester Docks

Liverpool

David was born in 1929 and spent his working life as a research chemist, initially exploring the synthesis of pharmaceutical compounds. On his retirement he took up photography, mainly of general landscapes but with a strong interest in darkroom and printing processes. He obtained his RPS Fellowship in printing and spent several years exhibiting his pictures worldwide. In common with many people, he was drawn towards black and white photography, having been inspired by Ansel Adams and, particularly, Edward Weston, who may have subliminally influenced David's sense of composition.

Although he photographs a range of subjects from quiet interiors to landscapes, there is a tranquil intimacy and deceptive simplicity to his images where the interplay of light and dark is of utmost importance. David has an intuitive sense of composition which regularly goes against conventional rules and which often allows the lightest part of the composition to be in the centre, allowing other elements to provide a counterbalance.

Historical methods of printing had always attracted him, in particular the use of platinum by workers around the turn of the century. The images shown here are a result of that interest. In 1832 Sir John Herschel reported that platinum compounds could be reduced to platinum metal by the action of light. This concept was taken up and developed over the next forty years and in 1886 Pizzighelli devised a method for contact printing large photographic negatives onto paper treated with platinum salts.

The final monochrome image registered the tones of the negative with extreme delicacy and ranged in colour from cold black to a very warm brown. One of the most active of the early platinum printers was Frederick H. Evans; his prints of British and European Cathedrals perfectly record the tone and texture of the subject. The most well known photograph is that of the steps in Wells Cathedral (ca.1900). Because of the vast increase in the cost of platinum this original process is rarely used.

The images in this portfolio are based on the same chemical principles but use materials more easily obtained and less costly. However David makes no claim to them being equivalent to the quality of the original platinum process. 35mm negative film is enlarged onto sheet negative film and then this positive image is contacted onto another sheet of film to give a final working negative of about 10"x8". At each stage, by selecting a suitable film developer, the contrast can be adjusted. If ortho film is used the work can be varied out under dim red light. The final print is obtained by contacting onto watercolour paper such as Fabriano 5, coated with a mix of palladium chloride and lithium chloride; effectively using lithium tetachloropalladate, with an iron salt as an activator. The image is obtained by exposure to high intensity UV light (black light) with exposure times in the range of 20- 40 minutes.

portfolio of work

david conway

The Way Up

Pot by John Leach

Cathedral

Control Tower

After an education in science and law, Mary pursued a career in industrial training and education development. Recognising that she needed an antidote to a very busy working schedule, Mary took up photography. Initially she only produced trade processed slides. However, in the early 1990s her style of work changed and a passion for producing monochrome prints quickly ensued. Much of Mary's most iconic work has been produced in the darkroom, but very recently she has made the decision to consider digital alternatives.

Despite her scientific training, Mary has always had a strong passion for the visual arts and in particular painting, sculpture and graphic design. Whilst her fascination with human nature has been the main driving force behind her photography, it is immediately apparent in the precise and balanced composition of her work that her awareness of the fine arts is a continuing influence.

In her early career as a photographer, Mary showed a strong sensitivity towards colour, but as her interest towards photographing people developed, she quickly appreciated that a limited colour range was required in order to lend greater emphasis to the spatial and design elements of the image. Portraying people in colour had never truly appealed to her as she was always striving for greater directness and simplicity. The transition from colour to monochrome was inevitable. Mary's instinctive appreciation of tone, the economy of her design, her meticulous understanding of lighting and her intelligent understanding of perspective are consistent features of her photography. She does confess that earlier in her career she did experience difficulty including figures in her photographs but, as her confidence grew, she quickly learnt how to overcome her reservations and now she hardly ever takes a picture that does not include a human element.

Her stated aim is to "take observational photographs in which I hope to capture never to be repeated slices of life". This usually requires working within an urban context, from both within and outside buildings, or wherever people are to be found. Mary never plans her work but aims instead to remain the dispassionate observer. She now has sufficient experience to be able to identify a potentially interesting location; she then discreetly waits for things to happen. What particularly fascinates her is "the transience of moments in time and the intriguing way in which people react to one another and their surroundings". Her capacity to capture these is almost unparalleled. She also acknowledges that her photographs make a statement about society and hopes that they may serve as an insight for future generations. Her overriding ambition is to create "pictures that transmit what I think and feel when taking them and to portray something of the human condition"

Because of the nature of her work, she keeps the equipment she uses very simple. With a manual SLR, just two lenses and filters, she has learnt to use her camera as an extension of her arm; mobility and speed of reaction are critical to her style of photography. Mary also emphasizes the need to work on her own; for her photography is not a social activity as it always requires her utmost attention.

portfolio of work

mary attfield

Mummy's Boy

Tired of Waiting

Life Cycle

First and foremost, Paul is a lover of the natural world and has been since his early childhood days. His photography is inspired by his affection and sensitivity for the beauty and moods of the landscape and, in turn, this fosters a deeper affinity and respect for the land.

For him the actual preparation and taking of the photograph is a very personal and emotional experience and this is the most important stage in the making of his photographs, as he attempts to capture his own response to what he sees and feels around him. His approach is not usually an immediate reaction to the landscape, preferring to allow himself time to identify and respond to the simple, the subtle and the intimate details that surround us all in the natural world, but which are so often overlooked and unloved.

The natural world is a very transient place; it seldom stands still. No two days are ever the same, and remaining in a place or returning to the same location or theme over and over again allows him to see and respond to this constantly changing landscape. On his first visit to a place he might only see the obvious, but by allowing himself the opportunity to return to a location he is able to tap beneath its surface, to discover its understated potential and, perhaps most importantly of all, to capture at least some of the soul of the place. Returning to a location means learning. It also means the chance to develop a deep love and passion for the places and subjects that he photographs.

Trees and woods are sanctuaries to Paul, and being surrounded by them enriches and cleanses his mind, his body and, most importantly of all, his soul. Allowing himself time is never more important than when he is in a woodland location, where he will often sit for a period of quiet contemplation before picking up his camera. This meditative approach allows him the chance to become completely at one with the place; not just to see what is around him but also to listen to the sounds, to smell the scents and to feel the spirit of the place. These are the occasions when he becomes completely at one with the landscape and when he feels most connected to himself.

Working more slowly as a photographer also allows Paul the time he needs to compose his images with great attention to detail, for it is important to him to get this right at the moment of taking and not at some later stage. The camera position is of extreme importance in these woodland situations, not only to ensure the most effective arrangement of the trees but also to make certain that any unnecessary detail and distracting highlight areas are excluded.

Paul also chooses carefully the lighting and climatic conditions to work with, usually preferring the beautiful soft and even light of an overcast day when bright highlights and harsh shadows can be avoided. Even more attractive are those days when moisture fills the air, whether it be a light drizzle or following a heavy downpour of rain, as this leaves the trees and the foliage fresher and more richly coloured. In his view, landscape photographers should never pass up the opportunity to photograph on an overcast, rainy or misty day.

Spending time alone surrounded by trees, and photographing them, has given Paul many uplifting experiences and precious memories. This is a passion that will last him a lifetime.

portfolio of work

paul foley

Pine Wood, Linn of Dee, Braemar

Birch Wood, Rannoch

Aspen Wood, Colorado

Ever since he can remember, Alan has been fascinated by the diversity and mystery of the natural world. Drawing and painting were early means of expressing this interest followed by photography in his teens. Aspirations for a career in art were frowned on by "elders and betters" resulting in a career in science teaching

His curiosity about the natural world was further stimulated by travel and the challenges of new environments. Alan delights in the contrasts between the Hebridean seashore and the wild coasts of Australia. He is as comfortable in the depths of a European forest as a Middle Eastern desert.

Frequently, his approach is to simply look and contemplate, arrested by the place, its atmosphere, the light perhaps or its silence. This "contemplative camerawork" as he calls it, is for him the vital experience: whether satisfying pictures result or not, the sense of connectedness with nature, contacting the numinous, the elemental forces of creation are enough.

Experiencing a musical performance can be intensely moving; without being able to explain it one just hopes that others sharing the experience will feel the same. So, in sharing the experience associated with taking the photograph, one hopes that others might catch a glimpse of what caused the picture to be taken.

A professional background in science has led Alan to follow developments in maths, biology, physics and ecology over the past 20 years, during which time there has been a synthesis in thinking to suggest a fundamental orderliness underlying the apparent chaos of natural phenomena.

There is a growing recognition that this 'orderliness' generates repeated patterns which are revealed in both living and inanimate matter at different scales; for example branching patterns in leaves, trees, roots, birds' feathers and river deltas. Waveforms occur so richly in nature that they have inspired artists in our own and other cultures such as Islamic and Aboriginal.

Alan tends to abstract detail from the broader view in order to create intimate landscapes. He thinks of his pictures as 'visual haiku' (the Japanese poem format}, examining the essence of the subject; combining apparent simplicity with a contemplative awareness of nature.

He has been using different modes of presentation to encourage the viewer to look again; pictures without frames printed on canvas or banner material, block mounting large prints (sometimes a metre wide) on watercolour paper and varnishing to avoid the need for glass protection.

Alan decided to follow an independent course and left the world of education for the precarious life of a freelance photographer. Having survived for over twenty years he is now concentrating on his art and has had several exhibitions.

portfolio of work

alan hayward

Bamboo

Reeds

Uluru

Iain first started taking photographs in his early teens, initially in monochrome, but increasingly in colour over later years. From the very beginning he tended to work thematically, presenting the resulting images in sets of individual photographs or as composite arrangements. Prime sources of inspiration for Iain were Gus Wylie's marvellous Hebridean photographs and, not surprisingly, the composite images and joiners of artist and photographer David Hockney.

It has been said on many occasions that a photograph cannot be viewed for long periods of time whatever its subject matter or quality of the image. Concentration soon begins to lapse and the need to 'move on' takes over. David Hockney suggested this 'viewing window' to be a mere 30 seconds after which time the viewer begins to lose interest.

It is possible to overcome this by presenting the viewer with a selection of images: a series of photographs on an isolated theme can aid the attention span considerably. Unfortunately this alternative is not always feasible, as exhibition space is often limited and magazine editors tend to operate with heavy demands on page allocation.

Another solution to the problem of retaining interest, without the need for a vast number of prints, is to construct composite images. These consist of a number of individual photographs based on a theme and generally displayed in a highly close-knit layout. By doing this the photographer can visually describe the subject in greater depth. Different angles, textures, details, colours etc can all be included within the one display and the viewer's attention can thus be held for longer.

The resulting composite collection demands extended viewing - there is an open invitation to explore all its many aspects. In certain instances, and by careful choice of images, the elements of time, space and movement can also be brought into play. What is essentially a still, two-dimensional medium takes on a new depth and life.

Finally, individual photographs illustrating small aspects of one particular scene can also be assembled in an overlapped 'joiner' to present the viewer with a made-up image of the original subject, another method first explored by Hockney and often featured in books and exhibitions.

Iain's portfolio opposite was inspired by a small abandoned corrugated-iron croft cottage of a type still found in the Western Isles of Scotland. What particularly attracted Iain was the general colouration of the painted and rapidly rusting ironwork and the textures of the deteriorating woodwork and exterior fittings. By grouping ten images, a photographic essay has been started, giving the viewer a far greater source of visual information on which to concentrate. The photographer has been able to show, in one simple collection, a range of colour, form, texture and mood that could not be presented in the standard single-image photograph.

The final composite of twenty-four images (on the next two pages 102 and 103) features old or abandoned boats and associated debris. The close-ups of peeling paintwork take on an almost abstract feel, contrasting with the clearly defined shapes, patterns and colour of the old timbers, ropes, chains, hawsers and netting. By presenting work in this way Iain aims to hold the viewer's attention and interest for a considerable length of time.

portfolio of work

iain mcgowan

It was being shown his father's new camera in 1980 whilst a student that first kindled Graham's interest in cameras. However, it was the discovery of a pile of 'Camera' magazines belonging to a friend's father a couple of months later that started a lifelong passion for photographic art, both as a practitioner and viewer.

A major catalyst in Graham's development was the Photographers Workshop that operated in Southampton in the 1980s and 1990s. An exhibition course run there by Mike Skipper proved to be the key that unlocked many working methods and techniques. Along with other members of this course, Graham set up the Image Workshop, a cooperative group that provided a critical forum for the development of its members, and a means of organizing exhibitions of their work. Since then, Graham's pictures have been shown widely at venues across the South of England, and exhibitions have been an important part of his photography.

Graham's work has always concentrated primarily on life as it is lived; the camera providing permanent witness to fleeting moments, moods and life's passage. In the past, this meant finding a likely location or event and working out the opportunities for meaningful images. These days, with a young family and a busy job, he has much less spare time and so now carries a pocket digital camera at all times to allow the snatching of images and thoughts as they occur during the flow of other things happening in life.

Both approaches have resulted in a portfolio of images that are far from project-based in outlook. Instead, common themes have developed that provide threads which link various subjects together. One major theme in his work is that of time. Many of his pictures are of fleeting 'decisive moments', the instant when form and content come to a climax. But there are other events which do not have to happen in an instant. Such images might show more seasonal variation, growth or decay. These apparently static moments are actually slowly changing and will vanish before their loss is noticed. Another major theme is that of relationships; of people themselves and their interaction with their environment. These pictures might manifest themselves as portraits, street pictures or landscapes of the worked countryside.

Stylistically, much of Graham's work is underpinned by tight geometric compositions, which have become simpler over time, especially for modern colour work. Surrealistic approaches and subdivisions of the picture space also help to present an image that invites inspection and re-interpretation by the viewer. Graham has used whatever technology has been available, but prefers a modicum of equipment. For many years this meant working on 35mm film and printing monochrome on fibre based papers. Today, without the darkroom, all of his work is shot digitally and printed using archival pigment inks, and because it is practical to do so, much of his work is now in colour.

portfolio of work

graham dew

Green

Lost Ball

Dandelion Clock

Harry Cundell strongly believes that age and occupation both have an influence on our artistic output. He spent nearly 40 frustrating years in banking and retired in 1978 at the age of 54.

Since then he has enjoyed a period of "absolute excitement and adventure", pursuing an interest which has engaged him since his youth. Freed from the constraints of work, he relishes the new challenges photography offers and if he feels a particular project makes few demands of him, he actively seeks out something new.

Since he started taking photographs 40 years ago he has always been inquisitive, searching for new ways to express himself; this has inevitably required experimenting with different processes, and developing further skills. He constantly asks himself "what is the end product to be this time?" An admirer of the Bauhaus movement and the work of the Surrealists, Harry has sought to find a visual parallel in terms of photography. Having acquired a simple digital flatbed scanner just four years ago, he quickly appreciated that this much under-valued piece of equipment could allow him to explore entirely new aspects of the visual world. He was particularly enthralled by the incredible detail he was able to obtain and the capacity to blend his digital capture with other visual sources.

Using software such as Photoshop, each individually scanned file can be amalgamated with other images at an extremely high resolution, yet retaining its own layer and identity. It is not uncommon for Harry to use up to twenty such layers in order to create the final image. In order to fully utilize the scanner's potential, it is not unusual for Harry to scan a 700 megabyte file for an A4 output. With this wealth of information, he is able to be critically selective yet still retain stunning detail. Having made an initial scan, he carefully examines his options then makes a further very specific selection governed by purely aesthetic considerations. This, in Harry's view, is the important creative input. There are, of course, various technical issues one needs to consider. At this level one needs at least a gigabyte of ram because it must be remembered that these are massive files and Photoshop itself needs its own share of memory. The advantage is that an image resulting from a flat bed scan is often much sharper than it is possible to obtain when using a conventional camera. As a simple case in point, many of his selected files will comfortably enlarge up to ten or twenty times without any noticeable loss of quality.

In this brief portfolio, Harry has used a sequence of scans from a variety of fruit and root vegetables as his starting point. In order to retain rich detail throughout, the quality of lighting is an important consideration. From past experience he had noted that using conventional flash proved far too harsh for this kind of work; by way of contrast the simple yet soft directional light one gets from a scanner is much easier to work with.

portfolio of work

harry cundell

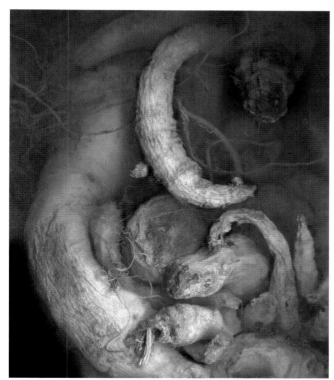

Held Together

Recliner

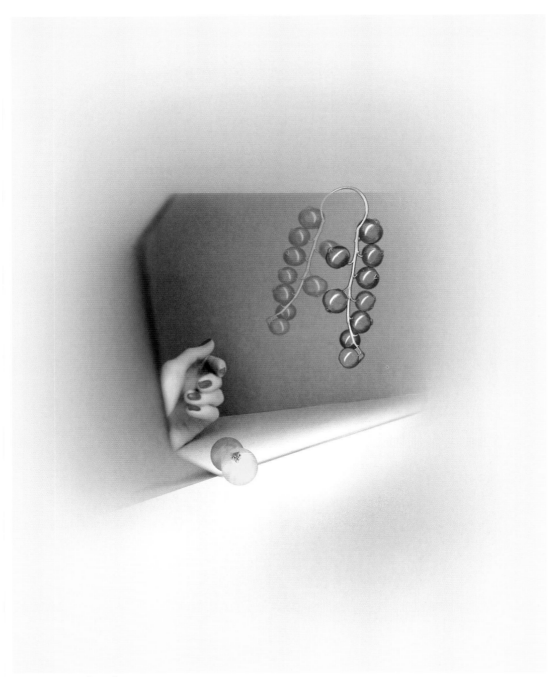

Mirror, mirror on the wall

Reaching out

John has a career background in education and his interest in photography began partly as an antidote to the pressures of managing a school. Although interested in photography prior to studying at university, it was not until the end of the late nineteen seventies that he had a real opportunity to pursue this further.

His photography, perhaps against current trends, is extremely wide ranging. Entirely self-taught, he relishes having broad photographic interests and works in a variety of mediums. As a consequence he has no wish to be 'pigeonholed'. His motivation comes from a desire to tackle a variety of subject matter and put his own stamp on it, whilst at the same time making it accessible to a wide viewing public. He works in both monochrome and colour with a preference for the initial image to be captured as a colour transparency. From this original transparency he currently produces both monochrome and colour prints. However, like many others, he is increasingly using digital capture when the situation demands.

Given the above background, it is perhaps not surprising that John cannot point to any single photographer as a major influence. Naturally, he can think of numerous photographers whose work he has admired; some of these specialize in the area of natural history or landscape, others are sports photographers or photojournalists. Probably, subconsciously, he has internalized their approaches but he would not put it stronger than that.

As well as pictorial and creative work and images taken on worldwide travels, he is an extremely active nature photographer with a particular love for Africa, a continent he has visited over twenty times. Living as he does in a major city, he particularly enjoys photographing in remote locations far from the bustle of western civilisation.

In the portfolio that follows, John has included a small selection of images from various locations around the world. These are places he has visited time and time again. With wildlife photography one can never be sure what might appear and whilst considerable patience is often required, the rewards can be substantial. The images seek to convey the beauty of the natural world and the creatures that survive, despite the destruction of vast tracts of their habitat. He hopes these images might make another small but personal contribution to ensuring that the planet is not destroyed by the pursuit of ever-higher living standards.

The images from Africa have been taken from a vehicle that is effectively a hide, with the camera resting on a beanbag. This gives a very stable platform on which to work. Typically the shots have been taken with either a 300mm or 500mm lens, sometimes with the addition of a converter. The other photographs have been taken by stalking the subject using a tripod and an appropriate lens combination. In all the images he has attempted to show aspects of the animal's behaviour set within their typical habitat.

As to the future, John is not too sure about what he wants to tackle next. Subject matter in the natural world is vast, and he is well aware from his own personal experiences that incidents in one's own life and in the lives of those close to us can blow one off course.

portfolio of work

john chamberlin

Elephant dust bathing

Pale Chanting Goshawk

Cheetah on Termite Mound

But finally we really must acknowledge the excellent work done by Ted Sturgeon who has given us so much of his spare time designing this impressive publication.

We are grateful to you all.

www.areanphotographers.com